NEEDLEWORK STITCHES

Barbara Snook

Needlework
Stitches

CROWN PUBLISHERS, INC.
NEW YORK

Library of Congress Catalog Card No.: 63-21112

ISBN: 0-517-025167
ISBN: 0-517-500795 pbk

Printed in the U.S.A.

Eleventh Printing, February, 1976

Contents

Introduction

In this practical, working dictionary of stitches, descriptions of method have been condensed or, in the case of the most familiar stitches or those with quite clear working diagrams, omitted.

Stitches have been grouped according to method and listed alphabetically within each group. Some may be found in slightly different guises.

Many of the foreign and possibly less familiar stitches are so interesting to work and so effective that the embroiderer who is willing to experiment with the wide variety of stitches illustrated here will be richly rewarded.

The material selected can alter the appearance of a stitch. Compare, for instance, Buttonhole and Satin Stitches used as Surface Stitches and worked on burlap, twill or homespun linen and when used as Drawn Fabric Stitches and worked on a loosely woven fabric. For counted-thread embroidery Hardanger cloth, evenweave linen, Aida cloth and Panama fabric are commonly used. In order to obtain the desired effect the thread or yarn used should be of a thickness suited to the fabric. Before beginning a piece of embroidery or needlework it is wise to test, on a scrap of material, any new stitch that has not previously been worked, experimenting with different threads to determine the best result. The chart shown below may be of assistance in matching fabric, threads and needles.

BARBARA SNOOK

FABRIC, THREAD and NEEDLE CHART

Fabric	Embroidery Threads	Thickness	Needle Size	Note
Organdy, muslin, voile, fine linen, lawn or sheer silk	Six Strand Floss	1, 2 or 3 strands	Sharp-pointed Crewel Needles	For working designs traced or transferred onto fabric.
Medium weight linen, gingham, rayon, silk, etc.	Six Strand Floss	2, 3, 4 or 6 strands	No. Strands 8　1 7　2 or 3 6　4 5　6	The number of strands of Six Strand Floss used depends on the requirements of each individual design.
Heavy linen, crash, etc.	Six Strand Floss	6 strands		
Huck Toweling	Six Strand Floss Pearl Cotton No. 5	6 strands —	Blunt-tipped Tapestry Needles No. 22 No. 19 or 20	For working over counted threads in Swedish Weaving, Cross Stitch, etc.
Heavy linen, crash, etc.	Pearl Cotton	—	No. 19 or 20	

Chart Courtesy Coats & Clark's "O.N.T." Embroidery Threads.

Bibliography

Anchor Book of Counted Thread Embroidery (Batsford)
Anchor Manual of Needlework (Batsford)
Canvas Embroidery and Design—Jennifer Gray (Batsford)
Danish Embroidery—G. Wandel (Batsford)
Dansk Hvidsom—Madsen, Winckler and Fangel (Copenhagen)
Dictionary of Embroidery Stitches—M. Thomas (Hodder & Stoughton)
Drawn Fabric Embroidery—A. Leach (Hulton)
Ecclesiastical Embroidery—B. Dean (Batsford)
Embroidery Book—M. Thomas (Hodder & Stoughton)
Encyclopedia of Needlework—Thérèse de Dillmont,
    Editions Th. de Dillmont, Mulhouse, France
English Smocks—A. Armes (Dryad)
Hardanger Embroideries, Series 1 and 2 (D.M.C. Library)
Hemslöjdens Handarbeten—M.Lundbäck, G. Ingers, E. Ljungkirst
    (Stockholm)
Let's Embroider—Heidi Haupt-Battagtia (Batsford)
Monster til Prydsom—A. Dyrkorn (Oslo)
One Hundred Embroidery Stitches (Clark)
Pohja-ompelua S-L Riuska (Helsinki)
Pohja-ompelua jagreikäompelua 2 (Helsinki)
Sammentraeksmonstre, Book 1 and 2 Waever (Copenhagen)
Samplers and Stitches—A. Christie (Batsford)
Smocking Books—Nos. 1 & 2 Penelope, William Briggs & Co., Ltd.
    Manchester
Sting og Monstre for Skole og Hjem—J. Arnbech-Jensen and
    M. Drejer (Copenhagen)
The Craft of Embroidery—A. Liley (Mills and Boon)
Wir erfinden Stickereien—M. and A. Leist (Basel)

8

SURFACE STITCHES

*Stitches used for free embroidery,
worked in various threads
on a wide range of fabrics*

Arrowhead

whether used as a line stitch or in vertical rows, should have the stitches worked at right angles to each other. It may also be used as a filling or a powdering, either alone or combined with other stitches

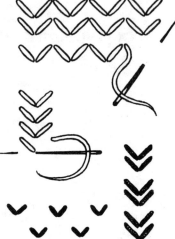

Back Stitch

must be small and perfectly regular. It is used for fine lines and detail, and is the basis of several other stitches, e.g. Pekinese, Dot stitch, and Interlaced Band

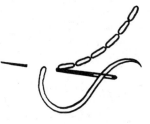

Back Stitch Varieties

a Threaded, single
b Threaded (double) produces a heavy line.
c Whipped—gives a slightly raised effect

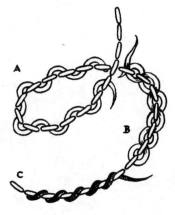

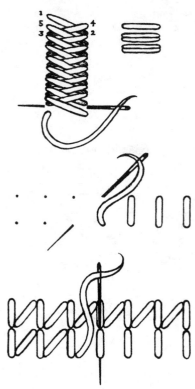

Basket

is a heavy, slightly raised line stitch. There should be closely worked parallel lines on the back

Bosnian Stitch

can be used as a line or filling stitch worked on the counted thread

Bosnian, Threaded

is a variation, worked in the same way as double running and akin to arrowhead in appearance. Compare with 'Sham' Hem stitch

Braid Stitch

is most successfully worked in a firm, unstranded thread. It should be compact for it quickly becomes untidy if too large or loose, thus destroying the slightly raised effect

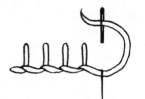

Buttonhole
is a versatile stitch used in many types of embroidery

Simple buttonhole or
blanket stitch

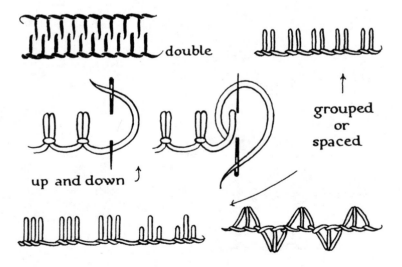

crossed buttonhole

↑
closed
varieties →

knotted varieties →

double

grouped
or
spaced

up and down ↑

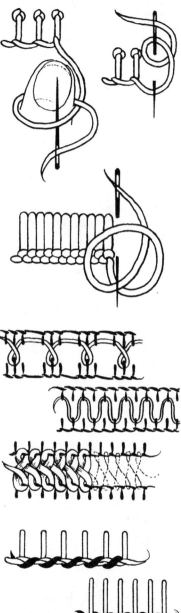

Buttonhole, Knotted
A knot is easily made by looping the thread round the thumb

Buttonhole, Tailor's
Stitches must be worked close together, whether used as a firm line or along a cut edge

Buttonhole, Threaded
Further variation can be made by using 2 threads of different thickness

Buttonhole, Whipped
Whipping from left to right gives a slightly different effect from working in the opposite direction

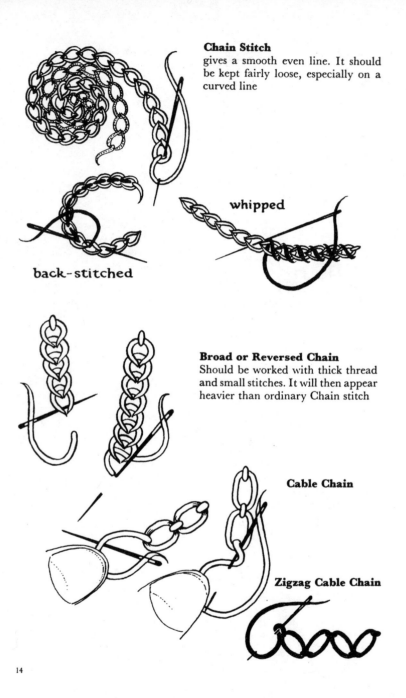

Chain Stitch

gives a smooth even line. It should be kept fairly loose, especially on a curved line

whipped

back-stitched

Broad or Reversed Chain

Should be worked with thick thread and small stitches. It will then appear heavier than ordinary Chain stitch

Cable Chain

Zigzag Cable Chain

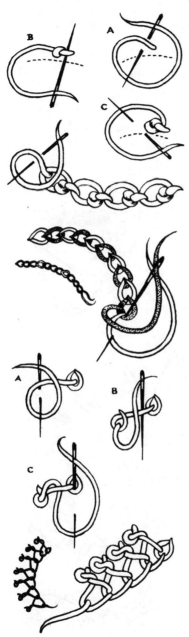

Chain, Knotted Cable
also known as Knotted Cable Stitch
This apparently complicated stitch is in fact easier to work than Cable Chain. A firmly twisted thread is needed

Chain, Chequered
also known as Magic Chain
Two colours are threaded through the same needle and used alternately. If worked carefully the unused thread slips back to the wrong side of the material. More than one stitch can be made before changing to the second colour

Chain, Crested
When the stitch is closely worked it forms a rich wide line. It is equally useful to give a delicate lacy effect on a curve

Chain, Detached
See also Link Powdering Stitch, p. 49

Chain, Double
is in appearance very similar to Closed Feather stitch

Chain, Heavy
gives an even wider line than Broad Chain. It must be worked with a firm thread. Make a small running stitch; bring the needle out just beyond it; thread back into the running stitch and insert the needle again where it emerged; take another small stitch forward and thread again through the first running stitch. Continue as in the diagram

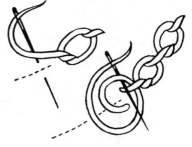

Chain, Knotted
makes a raised knotted line if worked with a firm thread

Chain, Open
A stitch which is more effective if ornamented.
See also Singalese Chain, p. 17

Chain, Rosette

gives a braided line if closely worked, or a petal-shape if openly spaced. It is effective on a curved line.

cf. Braid Stitch, p. 11

Chain, Russian

A light-weight border composed of groups of 3 Chain stitches

Chain, Singalese

Open chain worked over contrasting threads which give a twisted effect on each edge

Chain, Threaded

Chain, Twisted

gives a slightly raised line.

See also Coral Stitch, p. 19, and Hem Stitch, p. 97

Chain, Whipped

The whipping thread, which may be different in colour and thickness, does not enter the fabric.

See also p. 14

Chain, Zigzag

may be worked very small and close together as a firm outline, or with long slender stitches. To ensure that it stays in place, the needle should catch the thread down each time it enters the fabric

Chain Band, Chequered

Two different coloured threads, through blunt needles, are plaited alternately on a foundation of straight stitches

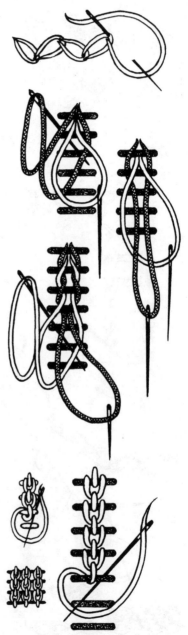

Chain Band, Raised

A composite stitch in which a chained stitch is worked, without piercing the fabric, over a foundation of straight stitches. These should be fairly close together to avoid stretching the chain

Chevron
is a line and filling stitch. In smocking it is used for surface honeycomb
See p. 106

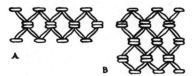

Chevron, Double (a)
Two rows of chevron, forming a diamond pattern

Chevron Filling (b)

Chevron, Raised
is a composite stitch worked on a foundation of evenly spaced V-shaped stitches. A thicker thread twisted through them produces a raised line, and only enters the fabric at the beginning and end

Closed Herringbone, *see* **Herringbone**

Coral
Similar to twisted chain with more space between the stitches, giving a delicate line

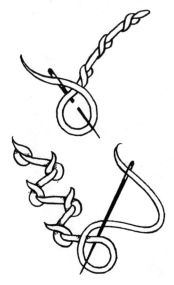

Coral, Zigzag
The stitches should be worked much closer together than in Coral stitch

Couching (a)

A thick thread or group of threads is sewn down with a thinner thread which may either match or be of a contrasting colour

Couching, Satin; or Trailing (b)

A group of thin threads is sewn down with a single thin thread using tiny Satin stitches, each taking up a very small piece of material

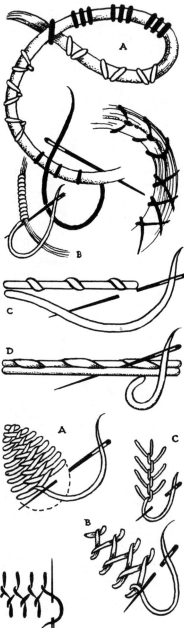

Couching, Bokhara (c)

may be used as a single line, but it is normally a filling stitch, when it may be used alone or with other stitches.
See Filling Stitches, p. 42

Couching, Roumanian (d)

is a filling stitch. It is shown here for easy comparison with Bokhara couching.
See Filling Stitches, p. 50

Cretan (a)

Cretan, Open (b)

In Cretan, the stitches may be worked close together or widely spaced. In either case they form a useful filling for small leaves or petals.

Both are good border stitches. The working method is akin to feather stitch

Long-armed Feather, (c) a form of Cretan.

See also Cretan Open Filling, p. 44

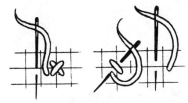

Cross

It is essential that cross stitch be worked by the counted thread on evenly woven fabric. It should only be combined with other counted thread methods, e.g. Holbein, Drawn Fabric and Canvas stitches

Cross, Single

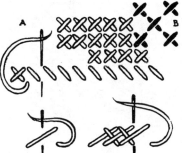

Cross, *for a line or filling* (**a**)
(**b**) *Spaced Cross Filling*
Spaced Cross Filling is worked in the same way as Cross when used for a line, except that the stitches are arranged alternately, with a space between each stitch

Cross, Long-armed, or Plaited Slav

On linen this is often the background filling for older forms of Assisi work

BACK

Cross, Marking

is worked so that it is neat on both sides. To achieve this, some stitches are covered twice

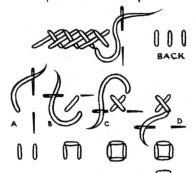

Cross, Two-sided

Four journeys are needed to complete one row. To make this stitch exactly the same on both sides, a half stitch is made each time the needle returns to the right hand side

Crown

Though the result is the same, the German (**a**) and Swedish (**b**) working methods are entirely different

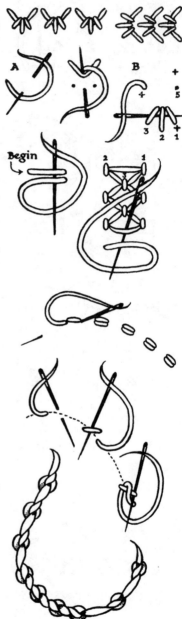

Diamond

A border stitch worked downwards. Make the first knot on the right hand side and a similar knot on the left. Insert the needle beneath it, make a third knot in the centre. Insert the needle again on the right hand side and continue the process

Dot

Two Back stitches are both worked into the same hole. Dot stitch can be used as a line or a filling.

See Seeding, p. 51

Double Knot

has a rounder, more distinctive knot than Coral stitch; when worked close together this gives a firm attractive line

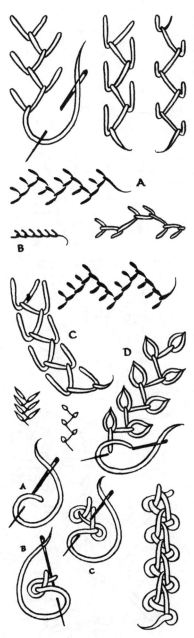

Feather

All Feather stitches have a direction and sense of growth and must be used with care. There are several variations. Feather was one of the main stitches used in the decorative panels on smocks.

See also Smocking Stitches, p. 105

Feather, Double (a)

Feather, Single (b)
is the same as Slanting Buttonhole stitch

Feather, Closed (c)
cf. Double Chain, p. 16

Feather, Chained (d)
is normally worked so that Chain and diagonal stitch are the same length. The zigzag line down the centre must be clearly defined and regular

Feather, Long-armed, *see p. 20*

Feather, Spanish Knotted
At first it is difficult to keep this stitch even. The secret lies in the diagonal angle of the needle. Once mastered, the result is a slightly raised decorative line

Fern
When used as a line, all three parts of the stitch are the same length. If it is used as a vein or leaf filling the outward strokes can be adjusted to the shape

Fishbone (a)
More often used as a close filling for small shapes than as a border stitch.
b Fishbone joining stitch, known also as Antique Seam

Fishbone, Open
More useful as a light filling than a line stitch. Its effect is similar to that of Leaf stitch

Fishbone, Raised
Used to fill small shapes which need to be embossed

Flat (a)
Sometimes known as Croatian Flat
b As a filling

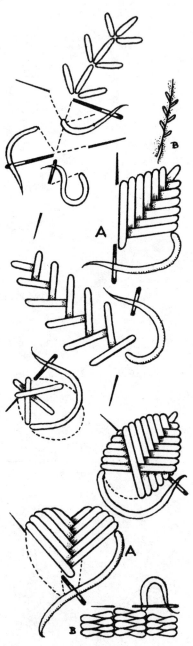

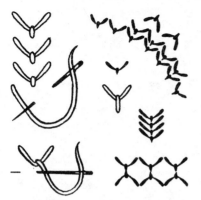

Fly

A very useful stitch which can be arranged in many ways. It combines well with other stitches to form border designs and all-over patterns

Guilloche

A composite stitch worked in 2 colours or 2 threads. Between parallel lines of Stem stitch work Satin stitch in groups of 3 stitches. With a thicker thread weave to and fro through these stitches; finally work a French knot in the circle which has been made

Herringbone

is the basis of many laced and threaded variations

Herringbone, Back Stitched

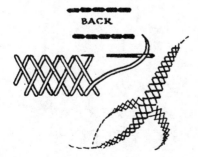

Herringbone, Closed

also known as Double Back Stitch
This stitch is quickly worked and gives a firm close line. In shadow work it is done on the reverse side of the fabric, producing 2 lines of Back stitch on the front, hence its second name.

In Drawn Fabric work it is also used on the wrong side to give a slightly embossed effect on the front.
See p. 81

Herringbone, Double

Two rows of Herringbone stitch are worked in contrasting colours so that they interlace

a Foundation for Interlacing stitch. It is most important that the interlacement is correct

b Both rows are worked as for ordinary Herringbone

Herringbone, Laced or German Interlacing Stitch

The small diagram shows that the needle is slipped *under* instead of over the thread

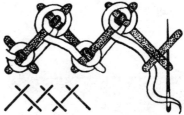

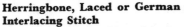

Herringbone, Threaded

The lacing thread, worked over a foundation of ordinary Herringbone, does not pierce the fabric. Try to avoid a join in the lacing thread

Herringbone, Tied

Over a basis of Herringbone, a zigzag line of Coral stitch is worked, often in a different thread

Holbein or Double Running

It is essential that an evenly woven material is used since Holbein stitch must be worked on the counted thread. It is completed in 2 journeys which, in a complicated design, need to be planned carefully to avoid leaving any spaces. Side shoots are best worked on the outward journey.

Note position of needle to ensure a smooth line. Holbein stitch is frequently used with Cross stitch and for the outline in Assisi work

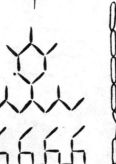

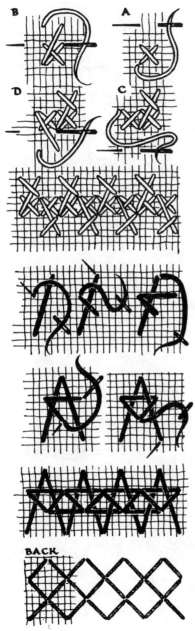

Insertion, One-sided

These stitches are confusingly named since they are not 'insertion' stitches at all and must be worked on the counted thread.

One-sided Insertion stitch is akin to Cross stitch

Insertion, Two-sided

This has the advantage of creating an even pattern on the back of the work

Interlaced Band

If worked on a basis of Holbein stitch instead of Back stitch, the interlacing can be done on both sides should the work need to be reversible. It should be on a fairly small scale to avoid too long a lacing thread

Interlacing

See also Maltese Cross, p. 57

In all interlacing designs of this type it is vital that the foundation threads be correctly arranged.

The finished pattern should be tightly knotted and compact.

A heavy twisted thread will give the best result

travel this way

begin
underneath

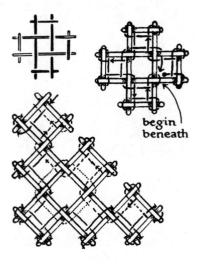

begin
beneath

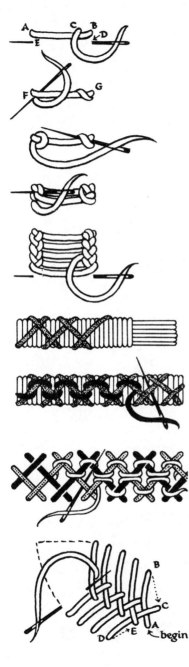

Ladder

A broad border with a plaited edge which may also be used as a filling for shapes of varying width.

It is embroidered towards the worker

Lattice Band, Raised

A foundation of long stitches is covered with Satin stitch, which in turn is crossed with Threaded Herringbone, forming a thickly padded stitch

Lattice Band, Twisted

Worked over a foundation of Double herringbone stitch. The interlacing is in 2 separate rows, only piercing the material at the beginning and end

Leaf

Although a fairly strong vein is formed, the edge is open and an outline stitch is usually needed to define the shape

Lock
An interlaced stitch on a foundation of straight stitches

Long-armed Feather, *see Cretan, p. 20*

Loop
Useful as a border stitch or a filling for small shapes. While making the loop the needle does not go through the fabric

Outline, *see Stem, p. 35*

Overcast, Straight
a Over a line of Back stitch, taking up a fragment of material
b Over Running stitch, near a raw edge, as in some types of applied work

Overcast, Detached
The overcasting thread is whipped over a foundation of loose Stem stitch, and does not itself go through the material

Palestrina
A closely knotted stitch

Pearl
When set close together a raised beaded line is formed. If spaced out the effect is similar to Coral stitch.

A fairly coarse thread gives the best result

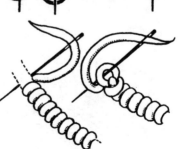

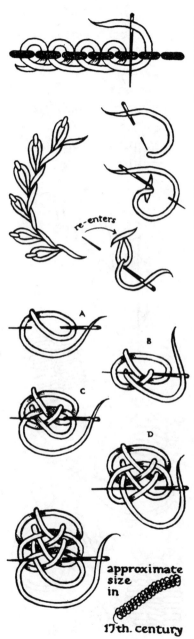

re-enters

approximate
size
in

17th. century

Pekinese

is worked on a foundation of small
Back stitches. A second thread is
looped through, with only a small
tight loop beneath the line.

Two colours or 2 thicknesses of
thread can be used

Petal

This stitch is most effective on a
curved line from which the Chain
stitches radiate

Plaited Braid

This complicated stitch was much
used in the sixteenth and early
seventeenth centuries, at that time
worked in metal thread.

A heavy thread is essential otherwise the loops tangle. The needle
passes alternately through thread and
fabric giving only small horizontal
stitches on the back. Experience will
show how loose to leave the loops

Portuguese Border

is worked in 3 stages. After the foundation threads are laid, 4 Satin stitches are made over the 2 lowest bars. The needle next emerges at **a** with the thread to the left of the needle, and makes 2 stitches over the first 2 bars, without entering the fabric. This process is continued to the end of the row. The second side is worked similarly, except that the thread is always on the opposite side of the needle.

Keep the surface stitches fairly loose

Portuguese Knotted Stem, *see* Stem, *p. 35*

Rope

The working method is similar to that of Twisted chain. The effect is quite different because the stitches are closer and longer, and the knot, which must be covered each time, gives a raised edge

Roumanian or Roman

A very useful stitch, either as a line or a filling for small spaces. It can often be used more successfully than Satin stitch

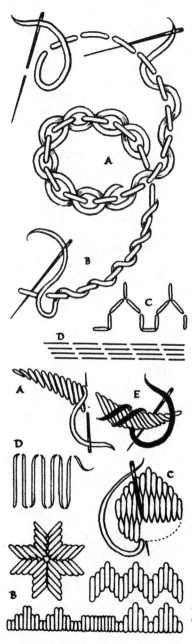

Running
A very simple stitch, valuable as the basis of several more elaborate stitches

a Threaded
Only a very small space should be left between the stitches

b Whipped
Further variation is given if running and whipping threads are of different thicknesses

c Holbein and **d Darning** are also forms of running stitch

Satin (a)
Satin stitch gives a broad line which can vary in width. It is very difficult to work perfectly

b Counted
Counted Satin stitch is, as its name implies, worked on the counted thread. It combines well with other stitches which demand an even weave fabric

c Encroaching
Encroaching Satin stitch is used as a filling for small shapes, and is a satisfactory shading stitch

d Surface
Surface Satin stitch is the basis for some couched fillings. As a filling it is more economical of thread than ordinary Satin stitch, but gives a less even surface

e Whipped
Whipped Satin stitch produces a fairly heavy, slightly raised line. Whipping stitches should cross at right angles to the foundation

Padded (no diagram), is worked as **a**, over several rows of Stem, Chain or Running stitch

Scroll

may be worked as a line or light filling. A firm thread gives the best result

Sham Hem

Worked on a zigzag foundation this stitch may be used as a border or as a seam decoration. The interlacing thread only goes through the material at the beginning and end of each line

Sheaf

A complicated stitch which needs a firm thread. It is always worked vertically upwards, in 3 stages, the first being a foundation of pairs of parallel threads. Long Satin stitches are then worked over the first and second bars, and still without entering the fabric, again over the second and third bars. It is most important that these stitches interlock correctly. A firm knot is next made, as shown in the diagram and this process repeated over each pair of interlocking Satin stitches. Each sheaf is tied with two Satin stitches as the needle progresses upward

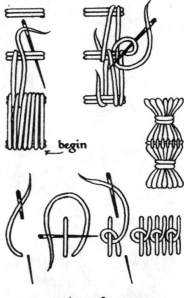

Siennese

A border stitch, worked between parallel lines

Slanting Slav

A line or filling stitch worked on counted threads

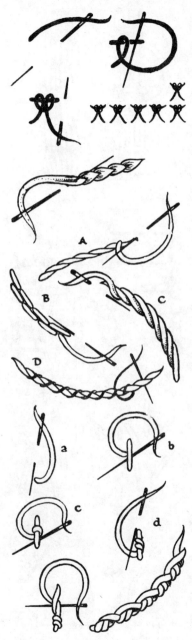

Sorbello

A heavy knotted stitch which comes from Italy where it is worked in a thick thread. The use of a thinner thread gives a light, very different result

Split

Split stitch should be worked in a frame, using floss silk. It can however, be worked in the hand with an even number of threads of stranded cotton, or with loosely twisted wool; great care must be taken to keep the stitch perfectly regular

Stem and Outline (a)

In Stem stitch the thread remains to the right of the needle, whereas in Outline stitch it is always on the left. In both stitches the needle enters and emerges on the line, each stitch touching; no space should ever be left between. Perfect Back stitch is formed on the reverse side of the fabric

b Alternating or Cable

In Cable Stem stitch the thread is alternately on either side of the needle

c Encroaching

A slightly slanting stitch is taken, just overlapping the previous stitch

d Whipped

The difference between Whipped Stem and Whipped Satin stitch lies in the much steeper angle of the Stem stitch. If a thick thread is used the underlying stitches can be completely covered

Stem, Portuguese Knotted

A raised knotted line most successfully made with a firm twisted thread

Stem Band, Raised

This is a Border stitch on a foundation of long, closely placed stitches, packed to raise the centre. These stitches are tied in position by horizontal stitches, evenly spaced. Then working from the bottom upwards, lines of Stem stitch travel across the horizontal stitches, always beginning and ending in the same hole giving rounded ends to the band. The foundation is completely covered

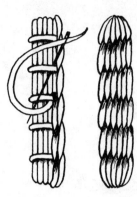

Step

Step stitch is worked in 3 stages, using a firm thread. Make 2 parallel lines of Chain stitch, with the stitches exactly opposite. Work a straight stitch into every other Chain stitch to join the rows. On the first bar, whip to the centre, make a slightly larger stitch, taking up a thread of material, continue whipping across and return through the back of material to emerge at the next bar. Whip to centre with needle pointing downwards, slip thread through centre stitch without piercing fabric, and continue whipping with needle pointing upwards

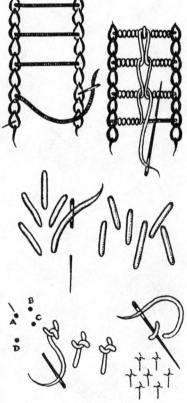

Straight or Stroke

This stitch consists of irregularly placed isolated Satin stitches

Sword Edging

may be used either as a line stitch or as a powdering. The lower branch of the 'sword' should be the longest

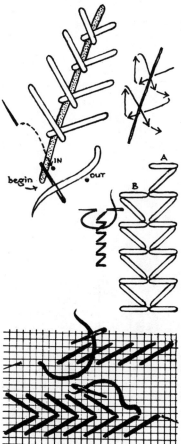

Thorn

Thorn stitch is a form of couching more easily worked with 2 separate threads than in the usual method of returning over a long stitch as in Bokhara couching

Triangle

Triangle stitch is worked in 2 stages. Row **a**, from base to top, then the work can be reversed for row **b**

Turkish, *see Three-sided Stitch, p. 93*

Two-sided Plaited Spanish

A border worked on counted threads, 5 along and 3 upwards. When the work is turned for the second row the thread must be secured carefully behind, because the needle has to come up again where it went down

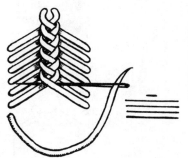

Vandyke

In the first stitch a small piece of fabric is taken up. Thereafter the needle slips through the loop and only enters the fabric at the sides, forming long horizontal stitches at the back

Wheatear

Wheatear is worked from the top downwards. The needle does not pierce the fabric when the chain loop is made

Woven Band, Diagonal

Woven band is worked from top to bottom over a foundation of horizontal stitches. Two needles are used, for contrasting tones. The threads twist with each other as shown in the diagram. Alternate rows are alike. Each thread must be long enough to complete the band without a join

Woven Band, Striped

The only difference between these two woven stitches is in the colour arrangement. Padding stitches can be placed beneath the horizontal bands to give an even more embossed effect

Zigzag

Zigzag stitch is worked in 2 stages, the crosses being completed on the second journey. An even-weave fabric is desirable

Unnamed Foreign Stitches

A Swedish form of Split stitch used in flower petals either alone or as a filling, when it is arranged like Long and Short stitch.

Generally there are 2 threads through the needle

Knotted Stitch
Danish origin

Buttonhole Stitch
German origin

Half Chevron
German origin

SURFACE FILLING STITCHES

*Involving materials similar to those
used for surface stitches, therefore
not including Canvas, Drawn Fabric,
and Drawn Thread fillings*

Arrowhead
for diagram and working method see p. 10

Back-Stitched Star
should be worked on even-weave fabric or coarse material, on the counted thread

Back-Stitched Trellis
An all-over pattern of lines of Back stitch arranged diagonally

Basket Filling
is a very close filling which gives a good texture if it is worked with perfect tension on the counted thread

Bokhara Couching, see p. 42

Brick
The first row consists of long and short Satin stitches, thereafter stitches must be of equal length, parallel and regular. The rows are worked to and fro. It can be used as a shading stitch

Brick and Cross
Groups of 4 Satin stitches may be vertical or horizontal. This filling is most easily worked in vertical rows beginning at the top. Two shades give further variation

Bokhara Couching

should be worked in slanting lines with the laid thread fairly slack and the sewing-down stitches tight. Avoid a tightly twisted thread which destroys the level surface

Bullion Knot Filling or 'Point Rose'

A filling which may be shaded. It is found in seventeenth-century work and is seldom used nowadays

Burden or Short Stitch

is a form of couching used in ecclesiastical embroidery. Spaced threads, laid horizontally, are held in place by vertical couching stitches. It may easily be shaded

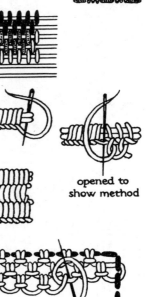

Buttonhole Filling, Detached

Apart from the first and last row, and the end stitch in each row, the stitches are free from the material. Even spacing, whether open or close, is essential

opened to show method

Buttonhole Filling, Fancy

A detached filling worked into an outline of Back stitch

Buttonhole Filling, Knotted

A detached filling worked into an outline of Back stitch or close Running stitches. In the diagram the link with the edge is shown large and loose for clarity

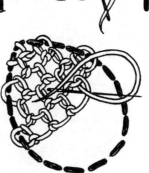

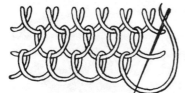

Buttonhole, Open

A detached filling, worked to and fro; apart from the first line, where small pieces of fabric are picked up, the needle only enters the material at the end of each row

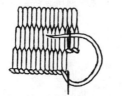

Buttonhole Shading

A very close filling, worked through the fabric; a suitable shading stitch

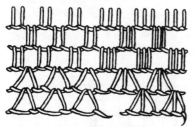

Buttonhole, Spaced

Stitches may be detached or pierce the fabric; many variations in spacing can be devised

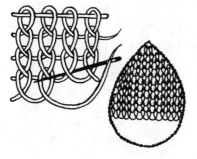

Ceylon

A detached filling which resembles knitting. It is more effective if not worked too tightly. Do not use a stranded thread

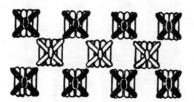

Chessboard

A large Cross stitch, secured by a small stitch in the centre, is worked over each group of 4 Satin stitches. One or two shades may be used

Chevron Filling, *see diagram p. 19*

Chevron-Stem

A frame should be used to ensure firm foundation threads. Over these, zigzag lines of Stem stitch are worked to form a close filling. Triangular spaces are filled in to complete the shape which needs to be outlined

Cloud Filling

A threaded stitch worked on a basis of alternately spaced isolated stitches, 2 colours or thicknesses can be used

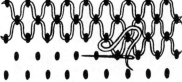

Couched Fillings

Couched fillings are capable of many variations in colour, tone and thickness of thread

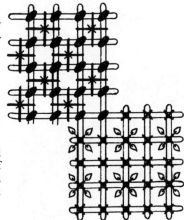

Cretan Open Filling

Cretan stitch is worked in diagonal lines over a firm foundation of straight stitches. It is only attached at the beginning and end of each row

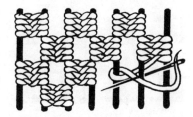

Cross, Spaced

for diagram and working method see p. 21

Darning
Only 1 thread should be picked up between stitches

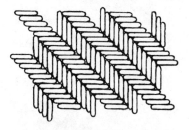

Darning, Damask
Stitches are of equal length and must be carefully counted. One direction is worked at a time. A careful choice of 2 shades can give the effect of shot silk

Darning, Double
Close rows of Holbein stitch, in which the stitches are the same length, produces the same effect on both sides of the fabric

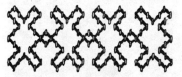

Darning, Huckaback
A threaded stitch worked on huckaback linen. Many different patterns can be devised. Ingenuity is needed to conceal the ends of the thread

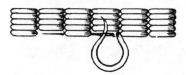

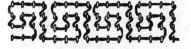

Darning, Japanese

This is worked on a foundation of darning stitches, equal in length and evenly spaced. A second journey links these stitches with a zigzag line

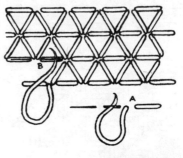

Darning, Patterned

By taking up and covering a different number of threads many patterns can be created. Care should be taken over the length of the stitches

Darning, Surface

A closely woven filling stitch detached from the fabric except at the top and bottom of a very closely worked Satin stitch foundation.

cf. Plaited Stitch, p. 50

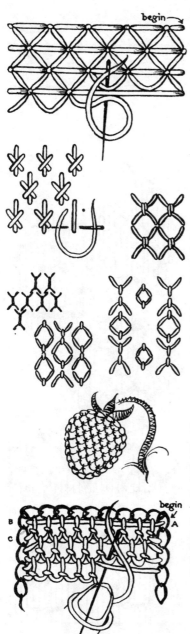

Diamond Filling

Lay a long thread from right to left across the space to be filled, bringing the needle out a thread below the line. Make a Coral knot and continue to the right, leaving a loop between each stitch. If a thread of material is caught each time it is easier to keep the stitch even. When one line is complete another thread is thrown across, starting a little way below, and the loop is tied to it as shown in the diagram

Ermine Filling

Stitches should be evenly spaced, with the crossed threads wider apart at the top than at the bottom

Fly or Crossed Fly Filling

Rows of Fly stitch are worked so that the tying down stitches are exactly side by side

Fly Filling

Fly stitch can be arranged in many ways to create heavy or light fillings

Hollie Stitch or Holy Point

Apart from the Chain stitch outline Hollie stitch is quite detached from the fabric. It is a lace stitch which was much used in the seventeenth century.

Begin at **a**, taking a long thread across to **b**, emerge at **c**, make a loop round the thumb as shown, and continue from left to right, throwing another long thread back when the end of each row is reached

Honeycomb Filling

A frame must be used for an even result. First lay the horizontal threads; place diagonal threads across from lower left to upper right, but do not interlace them. A third set of threads is laid diagonally across at right angles to the second set and forms the closely locked interlacement

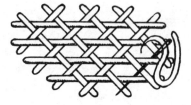

Laidwork

Although the richest effect is achieved with silk, other threads can be used successfully alone or combined, e.g. crewel wool may be tied down with silk. A frame must be used. The laid threads are in fairly loose surface Satin stitch

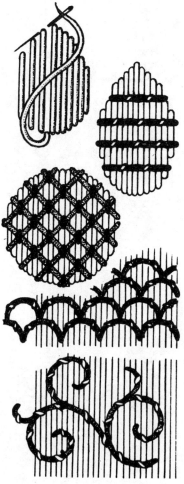

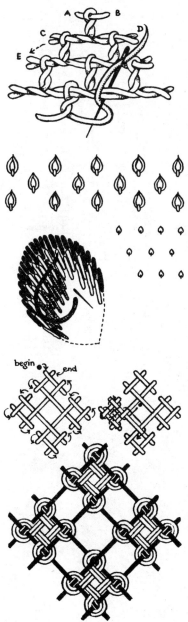

Lace Filling

Make a single stitch **a–b**, emerging at **c**. Form a twisted loop as shown, then take up a small piece of material at **d** before twisting the thread back to **c**. Re-emerge at **e**, proceeding as before. There should be only one twist for each stitch on the return journey, and only the final row catches into the material. An outline is necessary

Link Powdering

A simple but effective all-over pattern is made with evenly spaced detached Chain stitches

Long and Short

This shading stitch is extremely difficult to work perfectly, even with a frame, for ideally, in the finished work individual stitches should be indistinguishable.

After the first row of alternate Long and Short Satin stitches which must have a marked difference in length, those of subsequent rows are equal in so far as radiation allows. This radiation of stitches is the main difference between Long and Short stitch and Brick stitch, though in the latter an unbroken surface is not expected

Maltese Cross Interlacing Stitch

Interlacing stitch motifs can be arranged to form a rich filling

Maltese Cross Filling

Interlaced Maltese Cross shapes are worked on a foundation of interlaced threads spaced in pairs. In forming the crosses, the second journey follows the same interlacement as the first

Plaid Filling

Two vertical and 2 horizontal stitches forming a cross are worked over a base of long interlaced threads. Two or 3 colours are needed to give a plaid effect

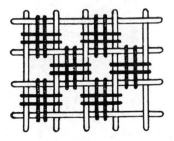

Plaited Stitch

See also Surface Darning, p. 46
This filling is most economically worked on a foundation of Surface Satin stitch. These threads are then darned in groups of three

Raised Honeycomb

A detached, very raised filling for which a fine thread must be used.

Work a detached trellis foundation without interlacing. Overcast first the vertical, then the horizontal threads. Twist over these the threads shown darker in the diagram and finally overcast the twisted threads, as on the bottom right hand side

Roumanian Couching

Both the long thread and tying down stitches should be kept fairly loose so that when finished the long slanting stitch should be indistinguishable from the laid thread.

cf. Bokhara Couching, p. 20

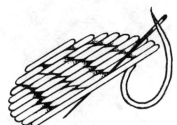

Roumanian or Roman Filling

There are many possible variations in the arrangement of small groups of Roumanian stitch to form different fillings

Seeding or Speckling

Many small back stitches (**a**) are scattered in all directions.

Dot stitch or Back stitched seeding (**b**) produces a heavier effect

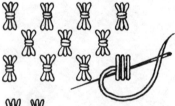

Sheaf Filling

Groups of 3 or 4 Satin stitches are tied in the centre by one or two stitches. This is usually worked as a powdering but long bunches can be overlapped to give a closer result

Sheaf-cross

A variation which may be used as a line or filling stitch

Sheaf-cross

Star Filling

A powdered filling of crossed stitches tied in the centre with a very small Cross stitch

Stem Stitch Filling and Shading
A very solid filling which may be shaded if necessary

Tête-de-boeuf Filling
A powdered filling composed of detached Chain stitches set between 2 straight stitches; it is arranged in alternate rows

Trellis Couching
Many different patterns can be created on a basis of interlaced threads. In Trellis couching the long threads are arranged diamond-wise. The working method is the same as in Couched Fillings

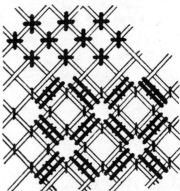

Trellis Couching with Herring-bone
Rows of Herringbone stitch are worked over a foundation of Trellis couching. The Herringbone may be tied down with Back stitch in another colour

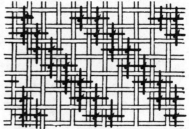

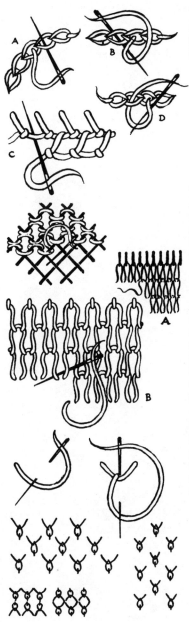

Trellis Filling
A very closely worked detached filling, linked into a Chain stitch outline

Twisted Lattice
A filling worked on the principle of twisted Lattice Band, either over the surface or in a cut square, in the latter case, the interlaced foundation threads must be close together

Wave Filling, Closed (a)
Open (b)
A shading stitch with nearly all the thread on the surface. It begins with a row of Satin stitches through which the next row is threaded, a very small piece of fabric being caught up to form the support for the next row of stitches. In Closed Wave all threads should touch

Wheatear, Detached
Detached Wheatear is usually a powdering stitch but can be used in many other ways. It is worked differently from Line Wheatear stitch

See also Wheatear, Detached, p. 58

pages 54–58

ISOLATED STITCHES

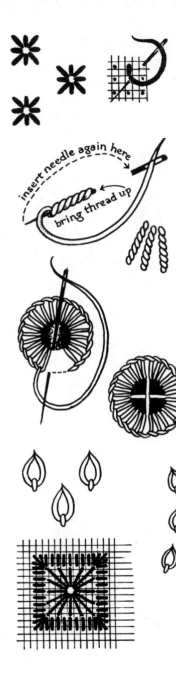

Algerian Eye or Star Eyelet
A Drawn Fabric stitch in which each star has 8 stitches radiating from the same hole. It may be used as an isolated stitch or worked in diagonal lines as a filling

Bullion Knot or Bullion Stitch
Use a firm thread and a thick needle with a small eye so that the thread can pass easily through the coils which must not be allowed to slip out of place at the moment when they are reversed into position.

A stitch which requires practice

Buttonhole Wheel
Buttonhole stitches are worked close together pulling the thread away from the centre. On some fabrics it is helpful to start the hole with a stiletto

Buttonhole Wheel, Barred
This is worked in the same way except that one set of cross threads is left in the centre

Detached Chain, or Link Stitch
Detached Chain may be used in various ways, including a broken line, and a powdering

Drawn Square
A Drawn fabric stitch consisting of an Eyelet stitch worked over 6 threads in each direction, surrounded by a Satin stitch border covering 2 or 3 threads

Eyelets, Detached

The rays of an eyelet must be worked regularly by the thread, but the number, of threads covered will be determined by the size which is needed. A final line of Back stitch makes a firm edge

Eyelet Hole

A small eyelet hole is made by overcasting the edge of a hole pierced by a stiletto. The beginning of the thread, run round this hole, gives sufficient padding.

Larger holes need a line of very tiny running stitches to mark the edge before the centre is cut. A small cut can make an unexpectedly large hole. Overcasting covers both cut fabric and running stitch

Eyelet, *on fine fabric*

This can be used as an isolated stitch or an all-over pattern.

A circle should be marked on the fabric. Twelve pairs of Back stitches, radiate from the centre hole. Begin with 2 stitches on the circumference, then 2 into the centre and return to the edge, continuing the process

Four-legged Knot

As the second stitch of the cross is made a Coral stitch ties it firmly in position. Four-legged knot can be used for a powdering

Raised Knot or Square Boss

Each arm of a Cross stitch is covered with a Back stitch to make a firm raised knot

(*Out of alphabetical order for easy comparison with Four-legged Knot*)

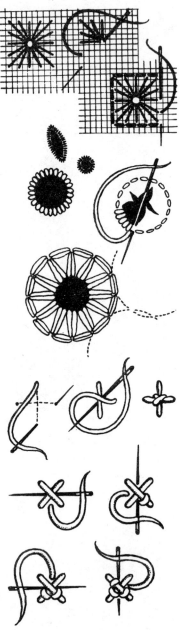

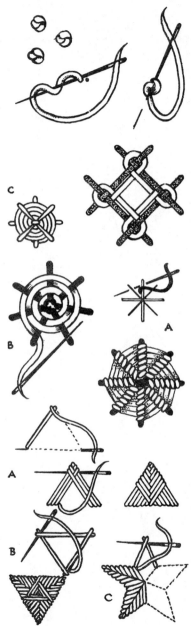

French Knot

Thumb and finger of the left hand must be above the fabric to hold the thread taut while the needle is twisted only twice round the thread. The needle is then turned completely to re-enter the fabric almost where it emerged.

French knots must be tight and resemble small beads. They are often used where Dot stitch would be more practical but if well made can be an effective powdering or close texture

Maltese Cross

See also Interlacing Stitch and Maltese Cross Filling, pp. 28, 49

Spider Web, Ribbed or Back Stitched (a)

A Ribbed Spider's web has an even number of foundation threads which are covered with a continuous line of Back stitch, starting in the centre, and travelling round until the desired size is made

b Spider Web, Woven

For correct interlacing an uneven number of threads is needed in the foundation

c Spider Web, Woven Wheel, or Woven Spot

Worked over an 8-spoke wheel

Sprat's Head (a), Crow's Foot (b) and Star (c)

Although these are tailor's finishes they can be useful in embroidery design where a strongly defined geometric shape is needed

Star Stitch

A useful isolated stitch frequently arranged as a powdering.

In Back-stitched star both the Back stitch and central cross can be worked in a finer thread

Tête-de-boeuf

A stitch which can be used as a filling, a powdering or as an isolated stitch

Wheatear, Detached

Detached Wheatear may be used as an isolated stitch, a powdering or in a variety of ways to form different lines and all-over patterns. Further variety can be obtained by altering the proportion of the chain and width of stitch

Woven Spot, *see Spider Web, p. 57*

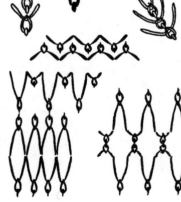

CANVAS STITCHES

Embroidery on canvas must cover the fabric completely. Since work is more interesting if it is designed for the use of several different stitches, it is essential that the thickness of the threads should be tested. Some stitches need a thicker wool than others if the mesh is to be filled, and if heavy cotton or pearl cotton are introduced the problem is accentuated.

When a motif is placed against an all-over patterned background, care should be taken that the latter does not dominate. Tone is particularly important in design for canvas embroidery

Algerian Eye

A very small stitch covering only 4 threads, 2 in each direction from the centre. The stitches are in pairs, making 16 for each eye. Rows are worked diagonally. The best effect comes with a fairly loosely woven canvas

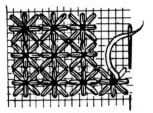

Algerian Plaited

Worked in the same way as Closed Herringbone. Though it appears the same as Plait stitch the method is different

Bricking

A form of Gobelin stitch, worked over 4 threads, leaving 2 between, so that the next row, beginning 2 threads lower, can interlock

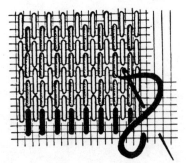

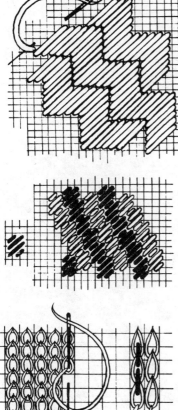

Byzantine
Satin stitch worked diagonally over 4 vertical and 4 horizontal threads in stepped rows, 6 stitches in each step. Useful for covering large areas of background. Two or more tones may be used if diagonal shading is required

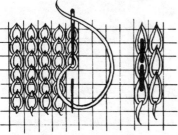

Cashmere
A background stitch giving a slightly irregular surface. It is worked from the bottom upwards, each diagonal row beginning 1 thread lower down

Chain
All rows are worked in the same direction, usually with each stitch over 1 thread of canvas. If a longer stitch is needed, 2 threads can be covered but Back stitch may then have to be added to hide the canvas

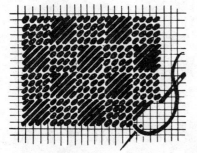

Chequer
There are 16 Tent stitches and 7 Satin stitches in alternate blocks, which may be worked in 1 colour or 2 tones of the same colour

Cross

Each cross should be worked separately. It is essential that all stitches should cross in the same direction, with lower left to top right being uppermost

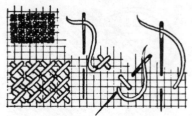

Cross, Diagonal

Worked diagonally from bottom right to top left. To cover the space which occurs between the rows, insert a small Cross stitch in a thinner thread. This improves the texture of the surface

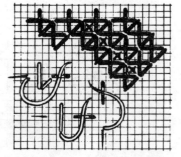

Cross, Half

Usually worked on double mesh canvas. Stitches should be worked very close together, completely covering the laid thread. The diagram is spaced out for clearness

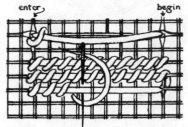

Large Cross and Straight Cross

A combination of 2 crosses to give a varied texture.

Work the large crosses over 4 threads and fit the straight cross between, over 2 threads

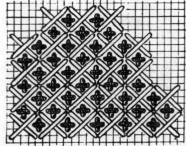

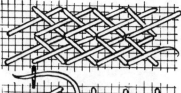

Cross, Long-armed, or Plaited Slav

A speedily worked stitch for covering large areas. It was used instead of Cross stitch in early Assisi work and in a similar technique in Moroccan embroidery

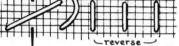

Cross, Montenegrin

This stitch is more useful on linen than canvas because the pattern made on the wrong side is also attractive and reversible

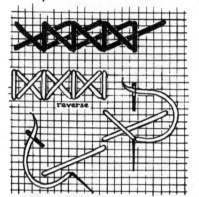

Cross Oblong

Unless it is further ornamented with Back stitch, threads of canvas are left exposed between the rows

Cross, Oblong, Back-stitched

The appearance of the stitch is improved if the cross is tied down with Back stitch

Cross, Reversed

Cross stitches are placed alternately straight and diagonal, and worked in diagonal rows. A finer thread is used to cross each stitch

Cross, Smyrna or Double

A Cross stitch is set diagonally with another cross worked vertically over it. Each pair is completed in turn. Two colours can be used to form a chequer pattern

Cross, Straight or Upright

Each stitch is worked over 2 threads of canvas with the horizontal over the vertical stitch. Each stitch is worked separately and the rows interlock

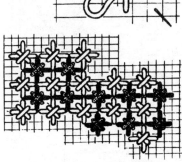

Cross, Double Straight

Straight cross, over 4 threads is held down by a smaller cross over 2 threads. The second row fits between

Cross, Two-sided Italian

There are 2 methods of working this small cross set within 4 straight stitches. In Method **a**, each stitch is completed in turn; in **b**, 2 journeys are needed for each row. The stitch which is alike on both sides, is useful on linen and in Drawn Fabric work

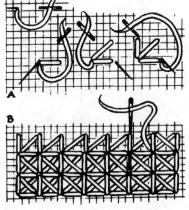

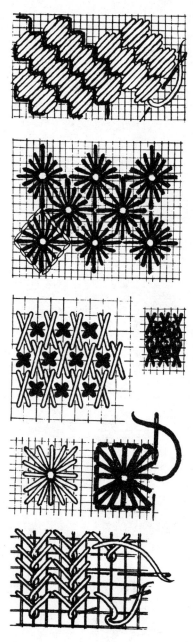

Diagonal

Worked from top left to bottom right. The Satin stitch rows can be divided by Back stitch

Diamond Eyelet

Worked from the centre outwards, over 4, 3, 2, 3 and 4 threads, continuing thus until the diamond is complete. A row of Back stitch can be worked between the diamonds if the canvas shows

Double Stitch

A combination of Oblong Cross stitch worked over 3 threads and Cross stitch over the thread between. It is worked from left to right. The diagram, which is spaced out for clearness, shows how the rows overlap. On a fine canvas it is easier to work over 2 vertical and 6 horizontal threads

Eye

Eye stitch can be used as an isolated stitch, as an all-over filling or as a border. It can be Back stitched for extra emphasis

Fern

Each row is worked from the top downwards. Provided the working method is adhered to, the number of threads covered can be varied according to the mesh of the canvas or the desired width of stitch.

See also Plaited Stitch, p. 74

Fishbone

Worked over 3 horizontal and 3 vertical threads, each long diagonal stitch is tied down with a short stitch across 1 thread. It should be closely worked

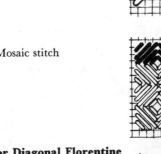

Flat

A form of Mosaic stitch

Florence or Diagonal Florentine

Worked in diagonal rows over either 1 and 2 threads or 2 and 4 threads

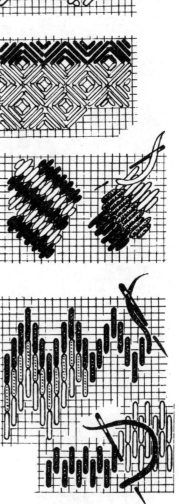

Florentine

From these 2 basic methods many intricate patterns, sometimes known as Flame stitch, have developed

Florentine or Flame Stitch

The apparently intricate designs of Florentine stitch are created by varying the length and number of the Satin stitches in each block

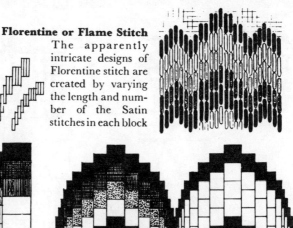

Generally each colour follows through, and while this is not absolutely essential for all rows, one at least should do so. Florentine stitch needs a large area in which to display its full beauty of shading and tone variation

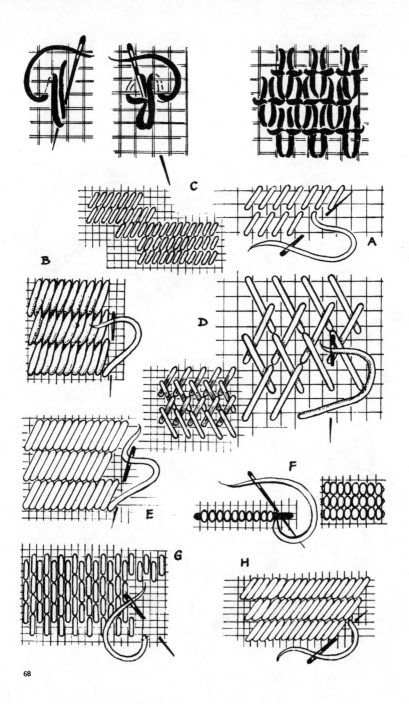

French
A very close stitch worked in diagonal rows from top left to bottom right

Gobelin (a)
b Encroaching
Worked in horizontal rows from top to bottom of the area to be covered. The stitch passes over 1 vertical and 5 horizontal threads. The next row begins only 4 threads lower, allowing for the encroachment of one thread

c Oblique
The same as ordinary Gobelin

d Plaited
Worked to and fro over 4 horizontal and 2 vertical threads so that the slanting stitches overlap those of the previous row

e Slanting
Worked over 2 vertical and 4 horizontal threads

f Straight
Satin stitch worked over 2 threads and a long padding stitch to hide the canvas

g Upright
Worked over 3 threads, leaving 2 threads between each stitch so that the next row can interlock.
cf. Bricking, p. 60

h Wide
Worked as ordinary Gobelin except that each stitch crosses 2 vertical and 3 horizontal threads

GROUNDINGS

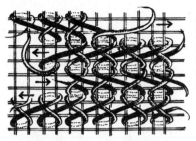

Greek
Lines are worked to and fro in a method similar to Herringbone stitch. The difference in direction in each row, of the long arm is the distinctive feature of the stitch

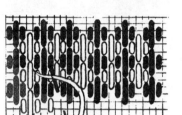

Hungarian
Worked in horizontal rows over 2 and 4 threads. Two colours or 2 tones of 1 colour may be used, or 2 different threads, but strong tone contrasts should be avoided

Hungarian Ground or Point D'Hongrie
Worked in zigzag lines and diamonds in 1 colour or 2 tones

Jacquard
This stitch is generally used for covering a large area. One colour is sufficient but 2 tones may be used. A row of Tent stitch is worked between each row of Satin stitch

Knitting Stitch

This appears to be Chain stitch but is in fact worked like Stem stitch, 2 rows up and down completing a pattern. Double mesh canvas should be used

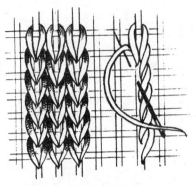

Knotted Stitch

Overlapping rows of slanting stitches, each tied down in the centre as in Roumanian stitch

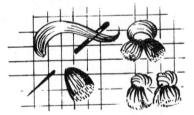

Knotted Stitch, Single or Tufted Stitch

This stitch imitates carpet knotting. Work the stitches between each other in alternate rows and use easily fluffed out wool. Cut the loops when the work is finished

Milanese

Worked in Back stitch in 1 colour. The diagram is shaded to show the arrangement of the stitches

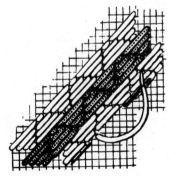

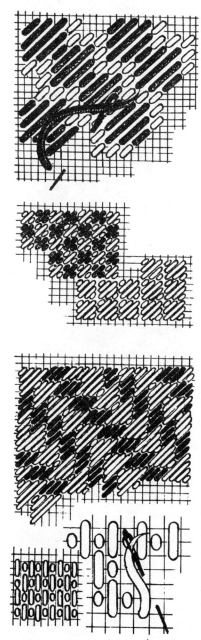

Moorish

A filling stitch for large areas. One colour or 2 tones may be used. Tent stitch is worked between the rows of larger stitches

Mosaic

A very small stitch which benefits from the use of 2 different threads

Oriental

A stitch which needs to be used over a large area to be seen to advantage

Parisian

A very close small filling.

> *cf. Hungarian and Mosaic, see pp. 71, 73*

It may be worked over 1 and 3 threads or over 2 and 4, in interlocking rows

Plait Stitch

may be used in successive bands as a filling. The needle only enters the canvas vertically forming a row of single upright stitches on the back

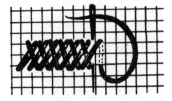

Plaited Stitch

is worked in the same way as Fern stitch, but with overlapping rows. It is easier to work each row from top to bottom

Ray Stitch

A simple filling which may be worked vertically or horizontally

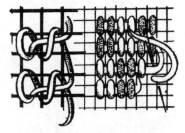

Renaissance Stitch

is worked in vertical rows in groups of 4 stitches (shaded for clearness). The wool must completely cover the canvas

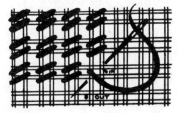

Rep Stitch

is worked in vertical rows on double mesh canvas, using both threads. If a thick thread is used, entirely covering the canvas, the stitch imitates the fabric from which it takes its name

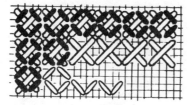

Rice Stitch

Work a ground of Cross stitch.

With a finer thread tie down each corner by working two horizontal rows, covering first the upper corners, then the 2 lower corners on the return journey

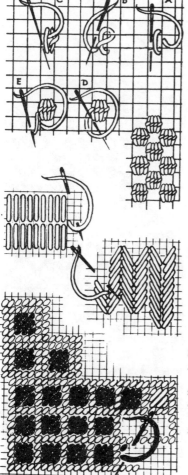

Rococo

A very attractive stitch if worked on a fairly open mesh canvas, care being given to the choice of thread which must not be too thick. The process is similar to Roumanian stitch, but because it is worked diagonally small holes are formed between each group of stitches. In the seventeenth century very small Rococo stitch was much used on samplers, worked in intricate patterns

Satin

Worked as counted Satin stitch

Scottish

A filling for fairly large spaces.

Groups of diagonal Satin stitch are set in an outline of Tent stitch. One colour is sufficient, but 2 tones may be used. A strong contrast is inadvisable

Shell

is worked in 3 stages; sheaves, coils, and finally Back stitch between the rows

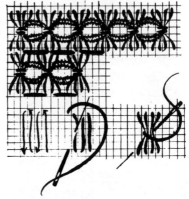

Small Chequer

A combination of Mosaic and Tent stitch

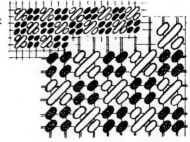

Star

Star stitch is similar to Algerian Eye, the only difference being that single stitches instead of double are taken into the centre hole

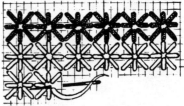

Stem

Worked from the bottom upwards over 2 horizontal and 2 vertical threads. When the surface is covered, spaces between the rows are filled with Back stitch, in a contrasting colour or thread

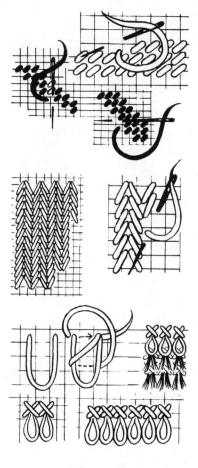

Tent Stitch or Petit Point

Tent stitch may be worked horizontally or vertically, but over a large area it is advisable to work diagonally to avoid pulling the canvas out of shape. The needle always goes back over 1 thread and forward 2 threads, making a longer stitch on the back of the work than on the front

Tent Stitch, Reverse

Worked in vertical lines, in alternate directions

Velvet or Astrakhan Stitch

All loops should be worked before any are cut. A wool which fluffs well will give the best pile

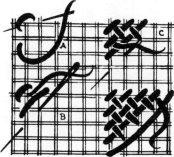

Web Stitch

Worked on either single or double canvas, Web stitch is a useful filling for very small areas. It gives a woven effect

DRAWN FABRIC STITCHES

Note: In a few instances the effect of the finished stitch is not easily apparent from the working diagram. Where this is so, a small sketch of the finished stitch has been included.

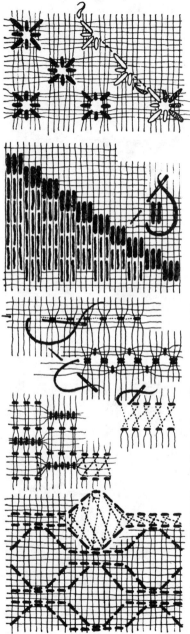

Algerian Eye or Star Eyelet
Worked in diagonal rows, with 8 stitches in each complete star

Algerian Filling
Worked diagonally, this makes a fairly solid filling, even with a medium weight thread

Back
Can be used alone, but is very often combined with other stitches. It can also be worked diagonally

Back, Double, or Crossed Back Stitch
A very useful stitch either alone or with other stitches. In certain arrangements it acquires another name, see Braid, Cushion, Double, and Ripple

Braid Filling
Based on Double Back stitch. Work from right to left, then turn the work for the next row. Pull fairly tight to make the 'cushion' stand out

Chained Border or Cable

This may also be adapted to a filling stitch

Chained Border, Diagonal

Showing a single row only, to give the direction in turning a corner. A second row is needed to complete the stitch

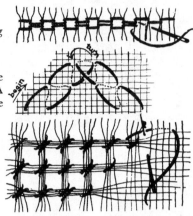

Chained Border, Filling

cf. Faggot, Reversed, p. 85

Chequer Filling

Made by 4 journeys across the fabric, covering 6 threads. If it is pulled too tightly the material puckers, and hard ridges are formed.

See Diagonal Cross, and Diagonal Raised Band, pp. 82, 83

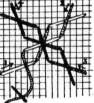

Chessboard Filling

A solid effect is produced only if a heavy thread is used. It is more attractive worked with a fine thread on loosely woven fabric

Chevron Cross Filling

A rather complicated stitch made of double rows of Cross stitch and double rows of Reversed Faggot

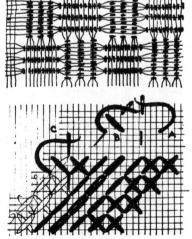

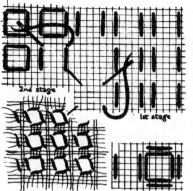

Cobbler also known as Straight Overcast Ground

Work all the horizontal rows of straight stitches, then turn the fabric and embroider as shown in the second stage, to complete the squares

Cross, Framed, Filling

The only difference between this and Cobbler is in the number of threads between the stitches

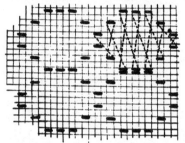

Cushion Filling

Based on double Back stitch, which should be pulled tightly enough to raise the cushion

Detached Eyelets

Other variations can soon be created by altering the number of threads to be covered with Satin stitch.

The smaller circle gives a good embossed effect if each stitch is worked twice, in a fairly heavy thread

Detached Square Filling

Work diagonally from the bottom right hand corner upwards, then turn the fabric and complete the squares

Diagonal Chevron Filling

Rows of Single Faggot are worked 3 threads apart; between each row, using the same holes, is fitted a line of Reversed Faggot

Diagonal Cross Filling

See also Chequer and Diagonal Raised Band, pp. 80, 83

A loosely woven fabric gives the best result

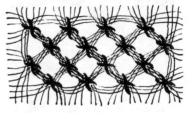

Diagonal Drawn Filling

Single Faggot stitch, with the rows 1 diagonal thread apart.

If more threads separate the rows, the effect is more open

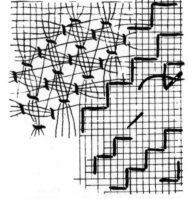

Diagonal Overcast Ground Filling

sometimes called Diagonal Whipped Stitch

This stitch is insignificant unless a Detached Eyelet is worked in each diamond-shaped space

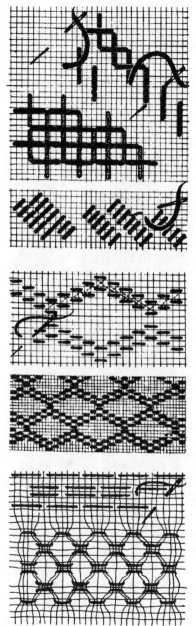

Diagonal Raised Band

Compare with Diagonal Cross and Chequer.

When pulled firmly the stitches make distinct diagonal ridges across the fabric

Diagonal Satin or Diagonal Whipped Stitch

A stitch which may be arranged in a number of ways, grouped or in a zigzag line. Its appearance varies considerably according to the thickness of thread and mesh of fabric

Diamond Filling

An arrangement of narrow lines of Closed Herringbone

Double Stitch

A filling based on Chained Border stitch. This method is used for *Reversed Wave* with a slight difference in the number of threads covered

Double Back Stitch

See Back Stitch, Double, p. 79

Drawn Buttonhole Filling

A lightweight filling of diagonal ridges in slanting buttonhole stitch. It may also be arranged in horizontal rows with very good effect

Eyelet Filling

A very close filling of eyelets worked with a single Back stitch on the outer edge and 2 stitches each time the needle returns to the centre

Faggot, Single

This may be considered one of the basic Drawn fabric stitches. It must be worked over an even number of threads, usually 4

Faggot, Double

is placed here, out of alphabetical order, because of its close similarity to Single Faggot, of which it is a development. It is Back stitched over only 2 × 2 threads making a dense filling

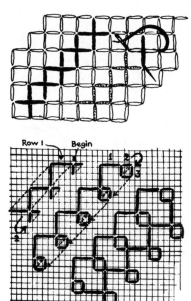

Faggot, Crossed, Filling

Cover the whole area with Single Faggot stitch, worked across 3 threads. Then work Diagonal Cross into the holes made by the Single Faggot stitches. These crossing rows can be arranged in various ways, alternately or at right angles

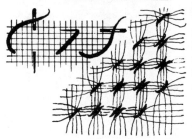

Faggot, Drawn, Filling

called Net Filling if worked over 3 threads

The filling consists of alternate rows of Single Faggot and squares. It is worked in 3 stages, turning the fabric for each stage. After working a row of Single Faggot return to the beginning, on the way making half each small square, which is completed when the work is again turned

Faggot, Reversed

This is the same as the wrong side of Single Faggot. *See also* Chained Border filling. If the work is turned and embroidered again in the opposite direction it is called *Russian Filling, see p. 92*

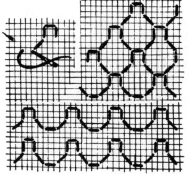

Festoon

Worked in Back stitch, festoon may be used in horizontal lines or arranged as a filling.

cf. Ringed Back Stitch and Waved Back Stitch, p. 91

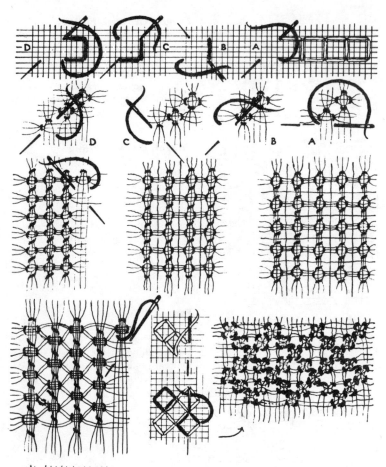

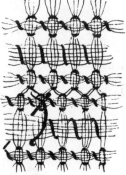

Four-sided

Four-sided stitch is a basic Drawn Fabric stitch.

It can be used as a border or diagonally, and for many fillings, either alone or with other stitches. Although seen at its best as a Drawn Fabric stitch, it can be worked successfully on all even-weave fabrics, in conjunction with other counted thread stitches and methods

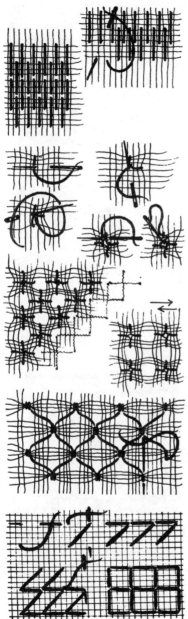

Gobelin Filling
A fairly close Filling stitch

Greek Cross Stitch
When used as an isolated stitch the ends are difficult to conceal. It combines well with Satin stitch, as a border

Greek Cross Filling
Greek Cross stitch can be spaced in several ways to make a delicate filling, which is usually worked diagonally but can also be worked horizontally. The method depends on spacing and arrangement

Honeycomb
A form of Back Stitch
cf. Wave Stitch which omits the Back stitch. A loosely woven fabric gives the best result. On firmer material a thread can be removed for the line of Back stitch

Italian Squared Ground
Worked from left to right on the *wrong* side of the material. At the end of each row turn the fabric and work back again. An extra stitch must be added to complete the square

Indian Drawn Ground

A filling or diagonal line stitch, most effective on transparent fabric. Rows may be worked in the same direction or back to back, in which case the fabric is turned round for the second row

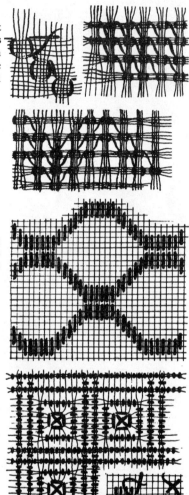

Lozenge

Worked in Satin stitch over 3 threads. It should not be pulled as tightly as other Drawn Fabric stitches

Maltese

After working 2 horizontal then 2 vertical rows of Satin stitch the squares are completed with Mosaic Filling stitch

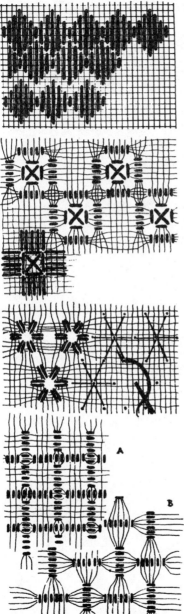

Mosaic Diamond

A close filling worked in Satin stitch. The diamond should be arranged to interlock, but the rows need not touch

Mosaic Filling

Four blocks of Satin stitch are worked to make a square which is filled in with a 4-sided stitch and a Cross stitch. This may be used as an isolated stitch, a border or a filling

Net Filling, *see Faggot, Drawn, p. 85*

Octagonal or Oblique Filling

The name is deceiving for the filling is made of 6 pointed eyelets with 2 Back stitches in each point

Open Basket (a)

Work all horizontal rows, taking the thread across the back of the space left for the vertical rows. If pulled too tightly it is impossible to work the second stage at each intersection

b is an unnamed stitch which is worked similarly, giving a more open result

Open Cross

A fairly solid reversible filling, worked to and fro from **a** to **b**, then across from **c** to **d**

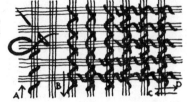

Open Trellis

A very light filling worked in the same way as Diagonal Cross, but with a different arrangement of the rows

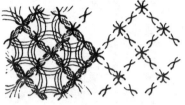

Pin Stitch

Pin stitch can be used in Drawn Thread and Drawn Fabric work, to hold down a hem and to secure thin material in appliqué work

Pulled Satin or Whipped Satin or Whipped Stitch

A basic Drawn Fabric stitch which is used in the formation of many other stitches. On loosely woven fabric numerous fillings can be devised

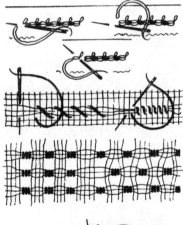

Punch

Work pairs of upright stitches in rows, to and fro. When the whole surface is covered turn the fabric at right angles and repeat the process to complete the squares. An even-weave material is most successful. On loosely woven material a large hole is made; the reverse side resembles Open Cross stitch.

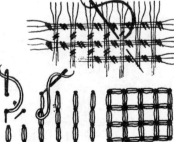

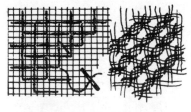

Ridge

This filling is the same as Diagonal Raised Band except that it is worked over 4 threads instead of 6

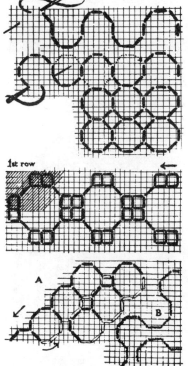

1st row

Ringed Back

A wave line is worked in Back stitch and the circle completed on the return journey. Ringed Back stitch can be used as a border or filling.

It can be combined with 4-sided stitch

Ringed Back, Diagonal (a)

Worked in 2 rows, with a single diagonal stitch in the first row
b Diagonal Waved Back stitch is also shown

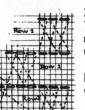

Ripple

Worked in Double Back stitch. Each row fits into the gap left between the blocks of the previous row.

This stitch does not stand out boldly unless a large quantity is worked.

Rosette Filling

A rich, rather complicated filling, which should be pulled tightly to raise the centre.

Follow the diagram carefully and proceed diagonally from one rosette to the next

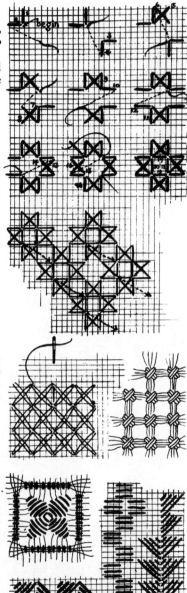

Russian Filling

When rows of Reversed Faggot stitch have been finished in one direction, the fabric is turned and the second set of stitches is worked across the previous rows

Satin

Satin stitch may be worked very tightly (*see Pulled Satin Stitch*), or in a slightly thicker thread than the rest of the work, with the stitches loose enough to form block patterns

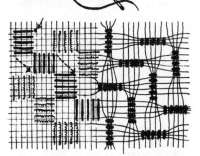

Stem, Broad
Used as part of a border treatment

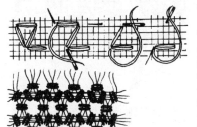

Step
Can be worked as Satin stitch, in a thick thread, or as whipped Satin stitch and pulled tightly. In either case follow the arrow in the diagram diagonally across the fabric

Three-sided or Turkish Stitch
also known as Bermuda Faggoting
The latter name is only used when the stitch holds down a small hem on fine fabric, or covers the join when one fine fabric is applied to another.

In Drawn Fabric work 3-sided stitch makes a tight heavy border and a close filling. It can also be worked diagonally

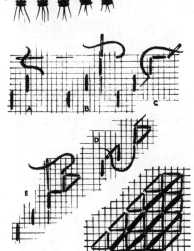

Triangular Two-sided Turkish
This reversible stitch gives the effect of a Drawn Fabric stitch. It is worked on the counted thread in diagonal stages, to and fro. The pattern formed is less distinct than the diagram suggests

Waved Back

Compare with Ringed Back.
For Diagonal Waved Back, see p. 91

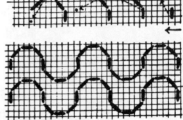

Wave Filling

Waved stitch gives a more solid filling than Window and Double Window for which it is the basic stitch

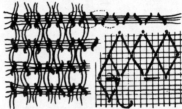

Wave, Reversed

If the work is turned over it will be seen that the horizontal instead of the vertical stitch dominates.
For method see Double Stitch, p. 83

Window Filling

The same method as Wave stitch, but with 1 thread left between rows; this thread completely alters the finished appearance

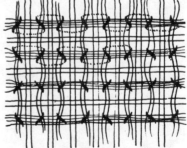

Window, Double, Filling

The same as Window, with 2 threads left between rows. The pattern is less distinct

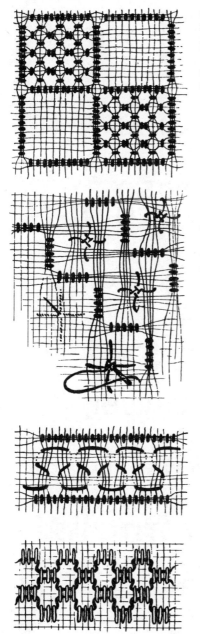

Four-sided and Whipped Satin Stitch

arranged in a chequer pattern is effective over a large area

Greek Cross Stitch and Whipped Satin Stitch

worked in diagonal lines; effective over a large area

Whipped Satin Stitch and Honeycomb Darning

Work all the Satin stitch rows before the Honeycomb darning

Threaded Satin Stitch

The Satin stitches should not be pulled too tightly. This filling is also successful with other counted thread stitches on evenly woven material

W.S

R.S

Drawn Thread Stitches

Hem Stitch, Antique
Worked in a similar way to Handkerchief Hem except that the needle is slipped between, instead of behind, the hem

W.S

Hem Stitch, Handkerchief
Draw out 2 or 3 threads. Hem stitch in small groups, only working on the side which secures the hem

R.S

Handkerchief Hem, *with Couching*
Several lines of couched thread can be worked close together to make an open border

Hem Stitch, Ladder
Remove 1 or 2 threads more than for Handkerchief hem. The groups are tied opposite each other

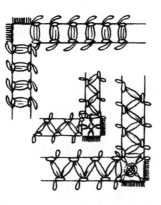

Hem Stitch, Serpentine or Zigzag
Enough threads must be removed to allow room for a clear zigzag line to be formed. Groups must contain an even number of threads so that they can be divided on the second journey

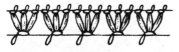

Hem Stitch, Bunched or Clustered

Hem Stitch, Clustered
Tied with Coral Knot stitch

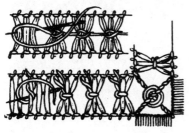

Hem Stitch, Clustered
Tied invisibly

Hem Stitch, Lattice
Work Ladder Hem stitch with a fairly wide space between the rows, to give comfortable room for the interwoven thread

Hem Stitch, Knotted Lattice

a After working Ladder Hem stitch the bunches are tied with Coral stitch, working from the back so that the chained stitch is hidden

b Shows that the wrong side of work is as attractive as the right side, and may equally well be used this way round

c Ladder Hem stitch is worked in groups of 2 threads. These are clustered in bunches of 4, using Twisted Chain stitch. A second row of Twisted Chain, worked in the same direction forms a zigzag line of divided bunches

d A slightly more elaborate version which looks better if Coral stitch is worked on the wrong side

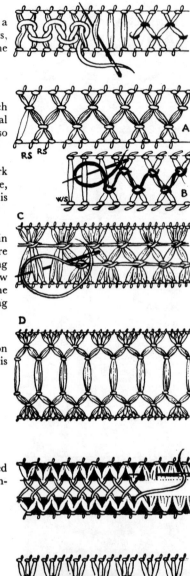

Hem Stitch, Double Border
Rows of Hem stitch are bunched alternately before the design is completed with Herringbone stitch

Hem Stitch, Clustered
and further enriched with overcasting and woven circles

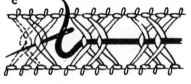

Hem Stitch, Interlaced

Worked on a foundation of Ladder Hem stitch

a The simplest type of interlacement

b Each bunch must have an even number of threads so that it may be divided

c and **d** both need a large number of threads removed to give the bunches sufficient play

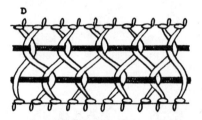

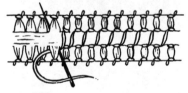

Hem Stitch, Italian

Two sets of threads are removed, leaving a similar number or a few more between. The outside is worked in Handkerchief Hem and the centre as shown

Hem Stitch, Woven

a shows a simple method of bunching the threads before weaving

b a woven border without an edging

Various Drawn Thread Work Border Stitches

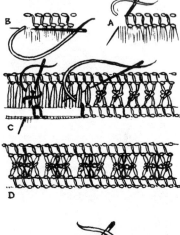

Fleur-de-Lis Stitch

Draw out 1 thread, leave 4, remove 6, leave 4 and remove 1. On this foundation work the top row as shown **a** and **b**

Begin the second row in the same way but before completing the second stitch, form a knot to join the 2 bunches of threads. If the knot is interlaced as shown, **c**, it will stay in place

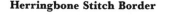

d Greek Cross stitch can be added between alternate bunches after the Fleur-de-Lis border is finished

Four-sided Stitch Border

Herringbone Stitch Border

Stem and Outline Stitch
worked after 1 or 2 threads have been withdrawn and the bunches formed by whipped stitch

Single Buttonhole Stitch
worked to and fro, to tie the bunches together after 2 threads have been removed

Chained Border variation

Chevron Stitch Border

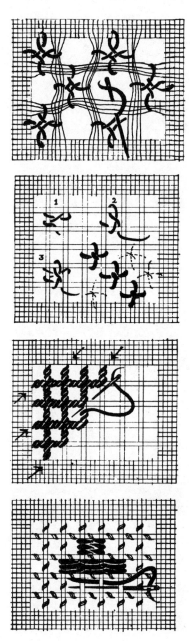

Drawn Thread Work Fillings

Greek Cross Filling

On a basis of 4 threads cut and 4 threads left, the rows are worked diagonally, so that in moving from one cross to the next the thread is hidden

Russian Drawn Filling

Cut 2 threads and leave 2. The 2 stages in the formation of the stitch are shown separately (1 and 2) and together (3). The pattern is worked diagonally downwards from top left to bottom right—the work is then reversed

Russian Overcast Filling, *also known as Russian Drawn Ground Stitch*

Cut 2 threads and leave 2.

Work diagonally, reversing at the end of each row. The openwork background is in strong contrast to the design which is of solid material in simple shapes, with firmly buttonholed or overcast edges

Weaving Filling

Cut 1 or 2 threads and leave 3.

Overcast all the horizontal threads before weaving, and all exposed vertical threads after the weaving is finished

Embroidery on Hexagonal Net

In embroidery on net the thread ends have to be darned in invisibly. The stitches are based on Running, Herringbone, Back and Satin, or a combination of these stitches, and not all are known by agreed names. If worked on square-mesh net, other terms are used, the method being called 'Lacis' or Filet Darning.

The following names are in use:

Back **q, r**

Chequer or Looped stitch (rows should touch), **a**

Cross, **e**

Diamond Filling, **l**

Diamond Eyelet, **o**

Eyelet also known as Lattice, **c**

Herringbone, **f**

Looped stitch (or Chequer), **a, k**

Ridge (Cross, worked horizontally or diagonally), **e**

Running, **j**

Satin, **h**

Slanting Back, **g**

Star, **l, n**

Stem, **i**

Threaded, **d, k, m**

Threaded, Wavy, **b**

Trellis or Lattice, **p**

103

Embroidery on Square-mesh Net

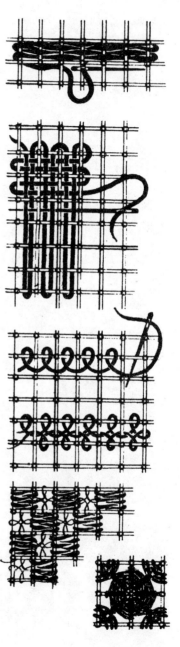

Filet Darning or Lacis embroidery is worked on square-mesh net; thickness of the thread used depends on the size of the mesh.

The 2 main stitches are Point de Répise or simple darning and Cloth stitch or Toile, double darning. Looped stitches and spider webs may be introduced

Point de Répise, simple darning

Cloth Stitch or Toile, double darning

Looped Stitch
may be called Ghost stitch

Greek Cross and Darning

Web Stitch

Smocking Stitches

These stitches are not arranged alphabetically, but are grouped according to similarity in method

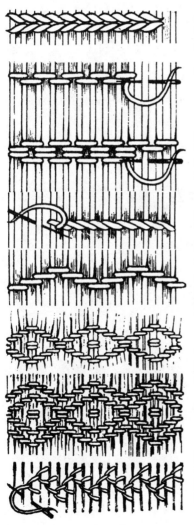

Outline
Worked in the same way as Stem stitch

Outline and Stem

Cable
Worked with the thread first on one and then on the other side of the needle

Double Cable
Two rows form the pattern

Wave
While making one set of steps the thread lies on one side of the needle, and is reversed for each part of the zigzag line

Trellis
Patterns made from different arrangements of Wave.
Both Wave and Trellis are tight stitches allowing very little stretch

Feather
Only if Feather stitch is worked very neatly indeed should it be used on smocking. It is a fairly tight stitch

Vandyke

A small tight stitch which should be worked much smaller than Surface Honeycomb

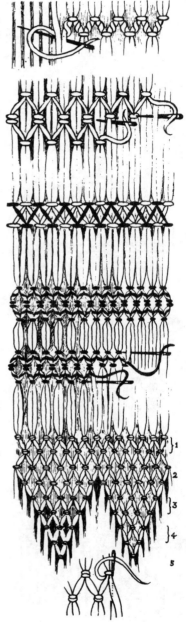

Diamond

Based on Chevron stitch. This is one of the larger smocking stitches

Crossed Diamond

Two colours can be used

Surface Honeycomb

A stitch with plenty of stretch. It works easily into points as shown in Honeycomb

Honeycomb

The rows of stitching are numbered to show how to avoid making the pairs of Back stitches fall on top of each other.

The thread passes within each 'tube' or 'pipe'

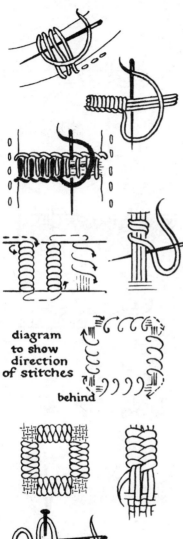

diagram
to show
direction
of stitches

behind

Bars

Buttonhole Stitch Bar
Throw long stitches across the gap
to be bridged. Work Buttonhole
stitch closely over these threads

Double Buttonhole Stitch Bar
Work a row of Running stitch along
the bar. Cover with spaced Buttonhole stitch, leaving only sufficient
space for the second row of stitches
to fit closely between them. The
fabric is cut away afterwards

Overcast Bar
Care must be taken that the thread
begins each time in the right place.
When forming the sides of a square
it is helpful to turn the work round

Woven Bar
Used in Woven Hemstitch and in
Hardanger work. The thread must
be taken behind at each corner if
making a square shape, to allow the
thread to begin in the right place

Buttonhole Bar with Picot
Used in Hardanger work and in
Richelieu work

Edging Stitches

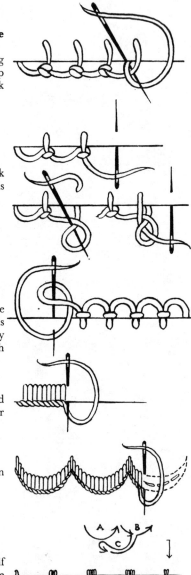

Antwerp or Knotted Buttonhole or Knot Stitch
Work from left to right as if making a Buttonhole stitch; over this loop make a Chain stitch. Use a thick thread

Armenian
Work from left to right, using a thick thread. Pull tightly when the knot is formed

Braid
Work from right to left, holding the edge outwards. As each loop is formed the thread is pulled away from the worker, a movement which helps to form a tight knot

Buttonhole
Ordinary Buttonhole stitch is used both for a plain edging and for scalloping

Buttonhole Scalloping
The stitches must touch to give an even surface

Ringed Buttonhole
Work the whole of loop **a** and half loop **b**; swing back to **a**; complete loop **c** and the rest of loop **b**. Use a firm thread

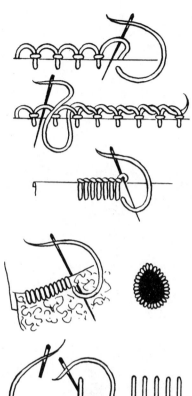

Hedebo Edging
Work from left to right, holding the edge outwards. As the loop is formed pull the thread out straight to make the small knot. The stitch is completed by whipping back to the beginning

Looped Edging
Worked over a small turned edge. The thread is brought through from the back and before it is pulled tight the needle is slipped through the loop and pulled away from the worker

Overcast Edging
A stitch used on the edge of small holes in Broderie Anglaise and as a joining stitch across the edge when lace is applied to lingerie

Plaited Edge Stitch
Stitches should be placed as close together as possible

Scandinavian Four-sided Edging
Begin on the wrong side of the fabric, working Stem stitch twice into the same hole to increase the size of the 'picot'. Turn to the right side; fold the fabric over with the small stitches on the extreme edge. Work a version of 4-sided stitch between them, pulling tightly. This edging can be used on an even-weave material or in Drawn Fabric work

Picots

In all Picots a firm thread is advisable

Bullion

Twist the thread several times round the needle and insert the needle back into the last Buttonhole stitch; continue the Buttonhole edging

Buttonhole Ring Picot or Ring Picot

See also Ringed Buttonhole Edging, p. 108

Take the thread back far enough to make a semi-circular loop when covered with Buttonhole stitch. Continue the Buttonhole edging

Loop

At intervals in a Buttonhole stitch edge, a small loop is made over a pin. When the loop is secure the pin is removed and the edging continued

Venetian

It is easier to form the picot if the Buttonhole stitch is worked from right to left

Woven

This is a fairly large picot which should be pulled tightly and worked with a firm thread

Small Unnamed Picot

Used on woven bars in Hardanger work

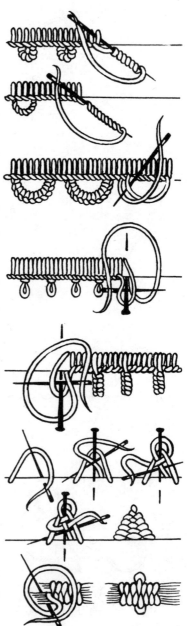

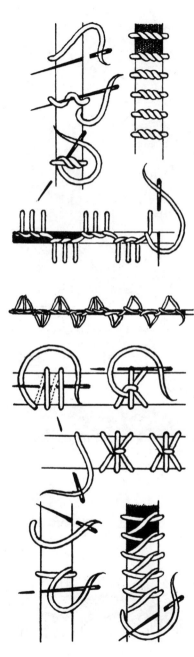

Insertion Stitches

An insertion stitch joins together two pieces of fabric which have been turned under to form a hem before being tacked the required distance apart on glazed linen, which holds them firm while work is in progress

Bullion Bar Insertion
Regular spacing and a firm thread are essential

Buttonhole Insertion
When changing from one edge to the other care must be taken that the joining thread is very tight. If it is allowed to stretch the groups lose their shape and become untidy

Diamond Stitch, *see p. 22*
May also be used as an insertion stitch

Faggot Bundles
Work fairly close together, with a firm thread, otherwise the stitch is not rigid

Half Cretan Insertion
Work the stitches very small and close together. A twist is formed only on one side. Compare with Open Cretan in which both sides are twisted

Interlaced Insertion
Worked on the same principle as Interlacing stitch, this makes a wide firm join

Italian Buttonhole Insertion
This apparently complicated stitch is quite simple to work and is by far the richest of all the insertion stitches. It is usually necessary to begin with buttonhole bar. The diagram shows how bar and the first group of Button-hole stitches are combined.

The stitches should be worked close together, the diagram is spaced openly for the sake of clearness

Knotted Insertion
Work as for Open Cretan, making a Chain stitch over each loop. When worked closely this is a firm stitch

Laced Insertion
This stitch can give an unstable result if the threads are not carefully chosen

Open Cretan Insertion or Faggoting
The working method is very similar to that of Feather stitch

Cretan and Buttonhole Insertion
This combination of 2 stitches gives an opportunity to use a second colour or threads of different thickness

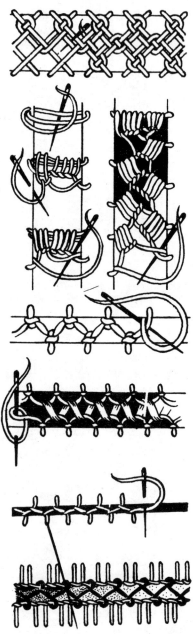

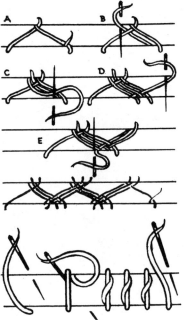

Plaited Insertion
A complicated stitch requiring perfectly regular spacing, and a firm thread

Reverse Roumanian Insertion
A loose stitch unless the thread is firm and only a narrow distance is left between edges

Twisted Insertion also known as Faggoting
A firm join if the distance between edges and thickness of thread are balanced

Whipped Buttonhole Insertion
An unstable join if worked loosely over any great distance

Cord
Though not an insertion stitch this is a means of joining together 2 turned edges

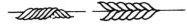

Abbreviations used in Indexes

Surface stitches	S
Surface fillings	SF
Isolated stitches	I
Canvas stitches	C
Drawn Fabric stitches	DF
Drawn Thread Work stitches	DT
Stitches used on Net Hexagonal	N
Stitches used on Square Mesh Net	N
Smocking Stitches	SM
Bars	B
Edging stitches	E
Picots	P
Insertion stitches	IN

Index to Stitches

Index According to Method

DRAWN THREAD WORK STITCHES

EMBROIDERY ON HEXAGONAL NET

EMBROIDERY ON SQUARE MESH NET

STITCHES USED IN SMOCKING